KU-273-639

Welcome to Jonah's Bible Adventure!

We're sure the kids in your life will love the journey they're about to embark on. From the great storybook and audio-cassette to the fun-filled activity book and interactive CD-Rom, your young adventurers will discover the story of *Jonah* in a new and exciting way. And the "Parents' Guide" will help you play a vital role in their experience.

Because what and how kids learn is important to us, we've had every element of *Jonah and His Amazing Voyage* reviewed by both a religious and an educational board of advisors. The content and vocabulary are appropriate for young children, and will help them develop reading and language skills, which are the cornerstones of education. Kids will also be able to expand and nourish their creativity as each Bible Adventure Club product challenges them to use their imagination. And most importantly, the knowledge they learn in these stories of God's Word will enhance their growing faith.

So begin with the great adventure stories of the Bible and start kids on a path that will enrich their lives in both faith and knowledge. And with you by their side, it'll be a fun-filled journey that you all will remember!

J onah was thanking God in his garden one day.

"You've been so good to me, God. If you ever want me to do anything, just ask me, and I'll do it."

To Temitope & Oluwatobiloba
Dada

from
aunty Sade Marwan
' 06

BIBLE ADVENTURE CLUB

Jonah
and his amazing voyage

janis hansen
illustrated by wendy francisco

CROSSWAY BOOKS • WHEATON, ILLINOIS
A DIVISION OF GOOD NEWS PUBLISHERS

ROBIN ROAD PRODUCTIONS
SHERMAN OAKS, CALIFORNIA

Dedicated
to all the little children of the world

OTHER BIBLE ADVENTURE CLUB STORIES

Creation: God's Wonderful Gift

Noah and the Incredible Flood

David and His Giant Battle

Jesus: The Birthday of the King

Jonah and His Amazing Voyage

Text and illustrations copyright © 2001 by Robin Road Productions
Published by Crossway Books, a division of Good News Publishers,
1300 Crescent Street, Wheaton, Illinois 60187

All rights reserved. No part of this publication may be reproduced, stored
in a retrieval system, or transmitted in any form by any means, electronic,
mechanical, photocopy, recording, or otherwise, without the prior
permission of the publisher, except as provided by USA copyright law.

Illustrations: Wendy Francisco
First printing 2001
Printed in the United States of America

Library of Congress Cataloging-in-Publication Data
Hansen, Janis (Janis S.), 1942-
   Jonah and his amazing voyage / Janis Hansen ; illustrated by
Wendy Francisco.
      p.   cm. - (Bible Adventure club)
   Summary: When Jonah tries to run away from God, he learns
the hard way that it is best to listen to God.
   ISBN 1-58134-329-9 (alk. paper)
   1. Jonah (Biblical prophet)-Juvenile literature. [1. Jonah
(Biblical prophet).
   2. Bible stories-O.T.] I. Francisco, Wendy, ill. II. Title.
BS580.J55 .H29 2001
224'.9209505-dc21   2001002269
                                                            CIP

15 14 13 12 11 10 09 08 07 06 05 04 03 02 01
15 14 13 12 11 10 9 8 7 6 5 4 3 2 1

Still, when Jonah heard God's voice, he was so surprised!

"Jonah, there is something I want you to do. Go to Nineveh and warn the people there. Tell them I will destroy their city if they don't stop doing bad things!"

Jonah walked into his home feeling very upset.

"Wife, God wants me to go to Nineveh and tell the people to stop doing bad things! I'm scared! Nineveh is not safe! Those people won't listen to me!"

"What will you do, Jonah?"

"There's only one thing I can do! I'll run away from God! I'll leave now! I'll go as fast and as far away as I can!"

Jonah grabbed a few coins, a loaf of bread, and some grapes and rushed from his home.

Jonah wanted to get as far from Nineveh as he could. He ran and kept running and running all the way to the seashore. He made his way to a ship that was loading cargo, getting ready to sail.

"Captain, I've got to get as far from Nineveh as possible! Where are you going, and when are you sailing?"

"Why, son, this must be your lucky day! We're going to sea within the hour, and we are sailing in the opposite direction from Nineveh! If you can pay me, you can come with us."

Jonah paid his fare and went down into the hold of the ship. He found a comfy spot inside a large coil of heavy rope, and when the ship set sail, Jonah fell into an exhausted sleep.

Of course, even though Jonah had traveled far, far away, God knew exactly where Jonah was. God sent a strong wind that whipped the ocean waves into a great storm.

The waves pounded the ship as if they would break it apart. The sailors tried everything to keep the boat from sinking!

"Throw cargo overboard! Lighten the ship!"

"We threw as much as we could over the side, and it did no good."

"The storm's worse than ever!"

"Find Jonah and get him to pray to his God to save us!"

Jonah was still asleep when the captain's men went below deck to get him.

"Jonah, wake up! How can you sleep through this storm? Quick! Come pray to your God to calm the sea!"

"God won't listen to me! The storm is my fault!

God asked me to go to Nineveh, but I was afraid and ran away! He'll never forgive me! Just throw me overboard! Save yourselves!"

"Jonah, the storm is worse! You must be right!
God of Jonah and of heaven and earth and sea, we don't want to harm him, but take Your Jonah back."

The sailors tossed Jonah over the side of the ship.

The storm stopped! The sailors
saw the awesome power of God,
and they began to pray.

Jonah was in the water only a moment when he was suddenly swallowed by a whale!

"I can't believe it! I've been swallowed!

It's dark and damp and fishy, too.
I could really use a lamp!
I'm in a whale of a fix,
A whale of a jam!
And I'm sorry, yes, I am!
If I did what God asked me to,
I'd be home now, happy as a clam.
But I'm stuck in a whale of a pickle, it's true,
So sorry I could cry, boo hoo.
Sorry, dear God, I truly am!"

After three days and three nights, God decided to give Jonah another chance.

God sent the whale toward land. The whale gave a mighty sneeze, and Jonah flew out of its mouth and landed on the shore.

"Oh, thank You, God.
Thank You for saving me!"

"Get up, Jonah! Go to Nineveh! Tell the people there to stop doing wrong."

"Yes, God. Right away! I have learned my lesson."

Jonah set off running toward Nineveh! He didn't stop until he reached the gates of the city!

The people of Nineveh didn't harm Jonah. Even the king came out to welcome him!

"Quiet, everyone! Let Jonah speak!"

"God has sent me to warn you! God will punish this city in forty days for all the bad things you people are doing!"

The king of Nineveh knew Jonah was right.

"Jonah, we will change, starting now!

We will spend the entire day going without food and praying to God.

We will follow God's teachings! Thank you, Jonah, for bringing us back to the Lord!"

Because Jonah finally kept his promise to God, the people of Nineveh were saved.

Jonah learned that God's way is the best way.